ROKEBY PARK PRIMARY SCHOOL

Why do we wear that?

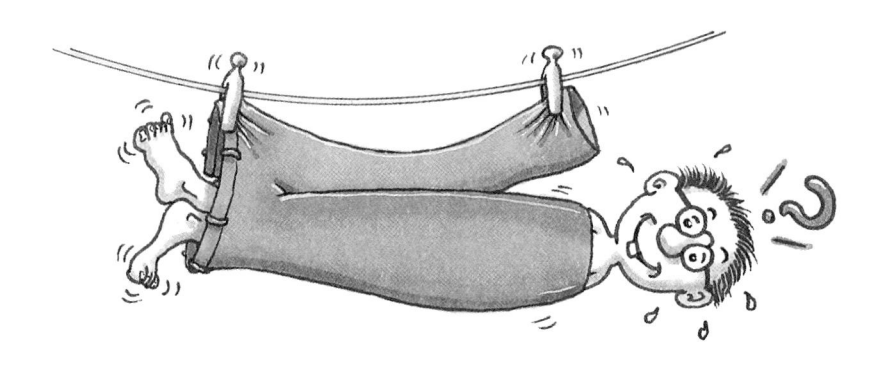

CONTENTS

Who needs clothes?	2
Shoes and boots	4
Underwear	6
Skirts and saris	8
Who wears the trousers?	10
Looking sporty	12
Jackets, shirts and waistcoats	14
Suit yourself	16
Posh dresses	18
Uniforms	20
Overcoats and gloves	22
Make-up, hair and tattoos	24
Jewels and things	26
Choosing a hat	28
Wigs	30
Quiz	31
Index	32

W
FRANKLIN WATTS
LONDON · NEW YORK · SYDNEY

WHO NEEDS CLOTHES?

Why do we wear clothes? After all, for many thousands of years, men and women lived in warm climates without clothes at all. So why did we suddenly decide to get dressed? People wear clothes for lots of reasons.

The way people dress can show which group or country they belong to.

Cowboy　　Rock musician　　Peruvian　　Farmer　　Businesswoman

There are practical reasons too...

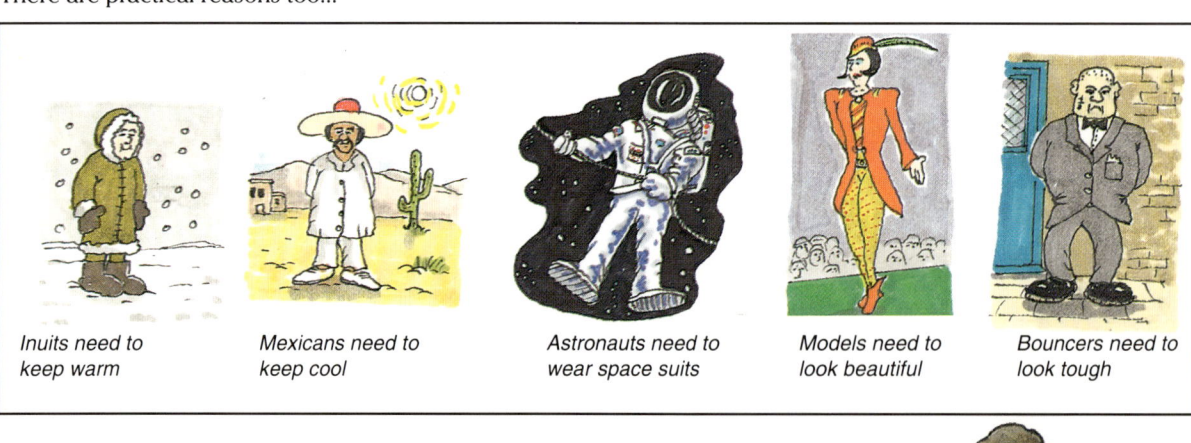

Inuits need to keep warm　　Mexicans need to keep cool　　Astronauts need to wear space suits　　Models need to look beautiful　　Bouncers need to look tough

Men and women have tended to dress differently, mainly because people expected them to. These days, however, we feel the differences are not so important. Sometimes men wear women's clothes, and sometimes women wear men's. There are also unisex styles.

Unisex safari suits, 1968

Revival of late eighteenth-century menswear, 1966

Different kinds of clothes are called styles. Because they are often only popular for a short while, they are also called fashions. If a fashion from the past becomes popular again, it is called a revival or 'retro'.

Throughout the centuries, a gradual broadening out of fashionable taste can be traced, from the aristocrats through to the middle classes and then to working people. In earlier times, attitudes to clothes tended to differ between the classes. Aristocrats were mainly concerned with show, the middle classes with respectability and the working classes often wore uniforms or practical working clothes.

Since World War II, young people have had more money to spend and, through television and magazines, they are more aware of clothes.

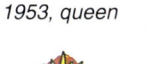

1953, queen

bank manager

newspaper seller

There have been many youth styles...

Teddy boy, 1958

Rocker, 1962

Mod, 1965

Hippy, 1969

Skinhead, 1971

Punk, 1977

Scientists agree that humans are related to the apes. Humans were once covered in hair. Then they began to migrate and had to adapt to different climates. Gradually, over many, many generations, humans grew finer and finer hair and became less 'furry', though nobody really knows why. This meant that when the weather was cold, humans were forced to find 'clothes' of fur to keep them warm.

The human body is capable of adapting to extremes of heat and cold. For example, some of the native people of Tierra del Fuego, in the far south of South America, lived in a cold climate, yet did not wear clothes. They carried a sort of woven mat that they held on the side of the body facing the wind.

In ancient times, wealthy Greeks believed that only slaves and barbarians wore a lot of clothes. They thought that it was unhealthy in a hot climate. They often wore only a large oblong of white cloth called an epiblemata. This was draped and folded round the body. The loose cloth sheltered the wearer from the sun and helped cool air to flow round the body.

SHOES AND BOOTS

For millions of years, people wore nothing on their feet. In some parts of the world, people still go barefoot. You could say they grow their own shoes. By walking or running on rough ground, they develop hard patches of skin called calluses, which make their feet tough.

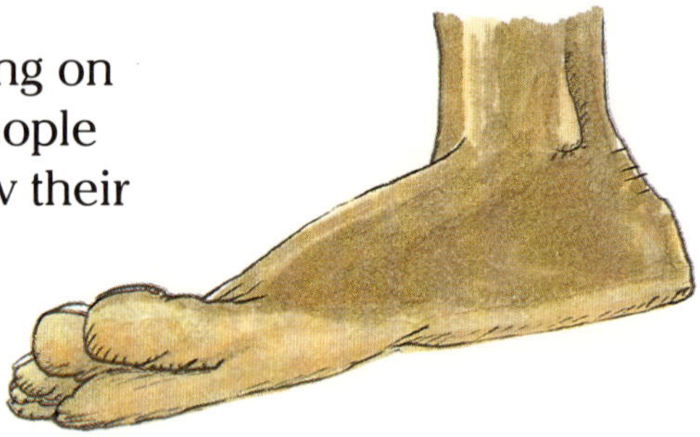

As civilization developed, people from powerful families spent less and less time walking outdoors on rough ground. Their feet became tender, so when they did walk outside, their feet would hurt. In ancient Egypt, noblemen would walk barefoot, followed by a servant carrying their shoes, ready for when they were needed.

Shoes became a sign of importance. Egyptian slaves and peasants were discouraged from wearing them. Egyptian shoes were often made from reeds or leather. Tutankhamen's tomb contained sandals. Pictures of his enemies were drawn on the soles, so he could tread them underfoot.

In Africa, some people make shoes out of old car tyres.

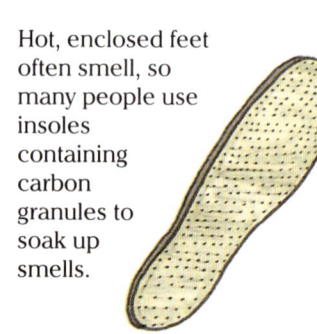

Hot, enclosed feet often smell, so many people use insoles containing carbon granules to soak up smells.

Balkan opanques are shoes with toe hooks. These are specially designed to grip the toe-bar provided on some non-Western toilets.

In rainy countries, it's important to have shoes that keep out water. The problem is that most waterproof materials also keep out the air. Feet need to breathe through the pores or tiny holes in the skin. Animal skins provide a good material for shoes, particularly if the leather is treated or cured, making it both flexible and waterproof but also allowing air to pass through. Skins were traditionally cured in urine – there are now modern substitutes.

Modern wellies are made of rubber.

From ancient times, boots have been used by soldiers for protection when marching across rough or wet ground. Wellington boots were named after the Duke of Wellington and were originally made of leather. They became very fashionable for men in the nineteenth century. The longer the boot, the more important the wearer.

Galoshes are rubber overshoes that slip over ordinary footwear.

A pair of cloth gaiters wrapped around the leg above the shoe or boot formed another form of leg protection. These helped to keep legs and stockings dry and warm in winter and were especially popular in the English countryside from about 1790.

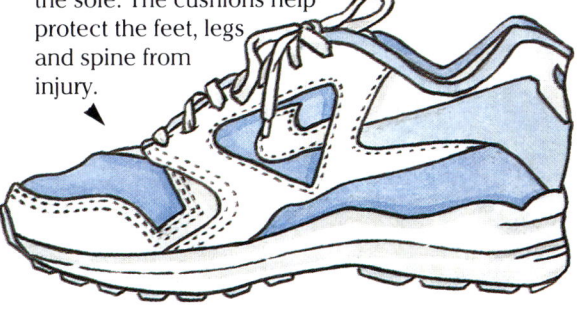

Clogs are wooden shoes that easily slip on and off the feet. They were popular in flat countries such as Holland and northern France, and with nineteenth-century British mill workers. In France, they are called sabots. People who threw their shoes into machines were called 'saboteurs'.

Sneakers are sports shoes with canvas uppers and rubber soles. They have steadily been replaced by trainers, which have leather or cloth uppers and air cushions in the sole. The cushions help protect the feet, legs and spine from injury.

High heels have been fashionable since the nineteenth century. They are meant to give height and improve the shape of the calf. Stiletto heels, very popular in the 1950s, damaged floors because so much weight was centred on two tiny spots. A similar shoe was fashionable for men in the seventeenth century.

Poulaines were long, pointed shoes worn in the Middle Ages. They had curling toes that could be up to 60 cm long and might be attached by strings to the knees.

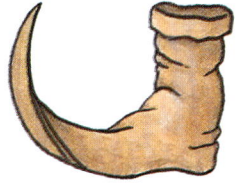

Winklepickers became fashionable in the early 1960s and got their name because they look like a tool for getting winkles out of their shells.

Stockings

Until the mid-twentieth century, women often wore silk stockings. These helped to make their legs look smooth. Nylon stockings were introduced in the late 1930s as cheaper alternatives. Women's stockings were kept up either with garters around the leg, or by suspenders attached to a girdle or corset that fitted round the hips. Men wore garters or suspenders on the leg to hold up their socks.

Nylon stockings were in short supply during World War II. Some women stained their legs with gravy browning and drew a line down the backs of their legs to look as though they were wearing seamed stockings.

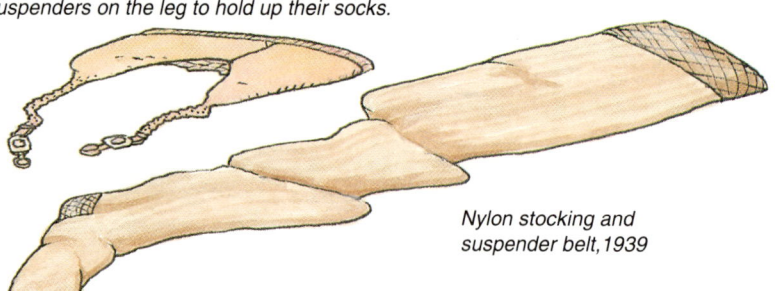

Nylon stocking and suspender belt, 1939

Underwear

It might be said that the first man or woman to wear one garment on top of another was the inventor of underwear. Now, we all use underwear to keep warm and clean, and sometimes to change the shape of our bodies.

Underwear helps to prevent dirt and smells from the body from reaching outer garments, which are normally thicker and harder to clean. Before the days of washing machines, people washed clothes by hand – scrubbing, rubbing, beating and shaking.

One of the simplest pieces of underwear for both men and women was the sleeved vest or undershirt. It hung from the shoulders and reached the hips or thighs.

Many men wear short-sleeved vests or singlets. However, in 1934, many American clothes shops reported a drop in vest sales after Clark Gable appeared without one in the film, *It Happened One Night*.

The T-shirt originated in America and was a simply-shaped vest. It is now worn as an outer garment by both sexes. It became fashionable after Marlon Brando wore one in the 1951 film, *A Streetcar Named Desire*.

The modern bra, or brassiere, was invented in France in 1912. It was formed from two handkerchieves and was often used to keep the body flat, because the new, working, professional women of the 1920s preferred a more boyish style of dressing.

At first bras were not firmly shaped. From 1936, however, semi-circular stitching gave the breasts a clearer shape. Wartime films began to show women with larger breasts. The film producer Howard Hughes designed a special bra for actress Jane Russell to wear during the filming of The Outlaw *in 1943. It made her breasts stick out more. The bra helped another actress, Lana Turner, to show off the shape of her body in close-fitting sweaters. She became known as the 'sweater girl'.*

Younger girls in the 1950s, however, found freedom with simple liberty bodices. In the 1960s, some of the new feminists burnt their bras as a protest against fashions which seemed designed only to please men.

In the 1980s, the singer Madonna wore a sharply pointed bra on the outside of her clothes to proclaim a more confident type of woman.

Corsets are designed to give women narrow waists. Sometimes men wear them too, either because they want to look slimmer or because they want to support a weak back. In the nineteenth century, women's waists were sometimes squeezed down to 45cm, which caused breathing difficulties, frequent fainting, crushed ribs and even death from damaged lungs.

In the nineteenth century, women were considered beautiful if they were S-shaped when viewed from the side. To achieve this, women needed their bottoms to stick out. They wore bustles (a sort of padded frame around the hips and bottom), sometimes adding crinolines – cage-like petticoats that made the dresses on top spread out. The tight-fitting corset helped to control the shape of women's breasts – flattening them or pushing them upwards.

Until the late 1930s, when Y-fronts appeared, men often wore long underpants of silk or linen. Pants, or panties, and briefs are now common for men and women, while men also wear boxer shorts.

Men and women used to wear linen drawers, or from the nineteenth century, the longer bloomers. Originally these were two separate tubes of cloth. French knickers, loose-fitting and fastened with a button, came into fashion in the 1920s. Sometimes they would fall down. It was said to be a sign of a true lady that if they did fall down she could carry on walking as if nothing had happened.

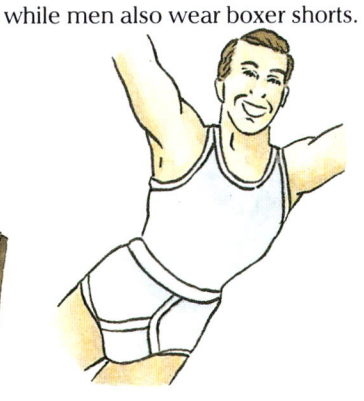

7

SKIRTS AND SARIS

Skirts have been worn throughout history, often by men as well as women. They are often shaped to fit the body, though some are simply wrapped around the waist.

Arabian haik

South Indian dhoti

Malaysian sarong

Many garments in warm countries simply wrap around the body. Such simple garments are easy to adjust and look elegant and dignified. Although the garments themselves are simple, great care is often taken over the kind of material used, the beauty of the pattern and the way it is wrapped and folded. Skirts are still worn by men as well as women in many hot countries. They are cooler than trousers, because air can circulate between the legs.

The Indian sari has been worn for at least a thousand years. It covers most of a woman's body, going right round the trunk and then over the shoulder, and sometimes over the head. The material is usually more than five metres long and over a metre wide. The Malaysian sarong is similar but is worn by men from the waist, and by women from the waist or the breasts down to the ankles.

Punk, 1977

Greek guard's costume

Scottish kilt

The Scottish or Irish kilt is really a short kind of sarong, made of thick woollen plaid, and containing many pleats. Other European men also wear skirts – guardsmen in the Greek army and a few modern city dwellers, such as the punks, who dress to shock.

Skirt lengths have changed frequently over the years. Rich women tended to wear longer skirts, while working women wore shorter skirts because they were more practical.

Skirt lengths tend to get shorter at times when women have more work, more money to spend and are more adventurous as, for example, in the 1920s and the 1960s.

English lady and peasant, 1350

1905

1925

1955

1965

8

The fishtail skirt (1877-1888) was so tight that an ankle-chain had to be worn to stop the wearer from taking large steps and splitting the skirt. Really fashionable women wore a chamois-leather undergarment beneath it, which allowed the knees to move only a few centimetres. It is not surprising that the fashion only lasted a few years.

Fishtail skirt

A man trying to shake hands with a woman in 1856 might have had difficulty.

Men and women have often tried to look as different to each other as possible. In the nineteenth century women took to wearing enormous skirts and dresses to exaggerate their femininity.

During World War II, short skirts in a simple, straight cut were worn by women who had to help the war effort and save on materials.

Local materials were once used to make clothes. Dresses made from tree bark were worn by some native Americans. Grass skirts are worn on some South Pacific islands.

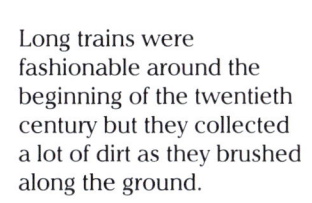

Grass skirt

Long trains were fashionable around the beginning of the twentieth century but they collected a lot of dirt as they brushed along the ground.

Soon after World War II, the French designer Christian Dior created a sensation with his 'New Look'. This featured wide, full-length skirts that were extravagant with material.

The short, straight skirts of the 1920s were a sign of women's growing independence. Short skirts shocked some old-fashioned people, who thought that women should remain covered up, and that short skirts were indecent. In Utah in the United States, women who wore skirts higher than 8 cm above the ankle could be imprisoned. In Italy, the Archbishop of Naples suggested that the earthquake at Amalfi was a punishment from heaven for those people who wore skirts that skimmed the knee.

In the 1960s, ordinary skirts first climbed above the knee and then rapidly shot up to the the thigh with the arrival of the mini skirt. When the model Jean Shrimpton, known as 'The Shrimp', appeared at the Melbourne Gold Cup horse race in a mini skirt in 1965, she caused a sensation. The popularity of the mini skirt was helped by the wearing of tights, which kept the top of the leg covered up. When the 1960s ended, skirt lengths fell rapidly.

1927: Oxford bags were wide flannel trousers worn by fashionable young men. The trouser bottoms could measure up to 120 cm round.

1956: drainpipe trousers were cut as narrow as possible.

1967: hipsters, or loons, were narrow and hung low on the hips.

1970: flares, or bell bottoms, were almost a revival of Oxford bags.

WHO WEARS THE TROUSERS?

Trousers have traditionally been worn by men, and men in the past have had more power than women in most societies. Trousers came to mean masculinity and therefore authority. The question 'Who wears the trousers?' used to mean which member of the family is in charge – the husband or the wife?

Breeches or knickerbockers were worn with stockings between the sixteenth and the eighteenth centuries.

Originally, men's trousers had a flap with buttons that came down in front, but this was replaced by the button fly. In the 1930s, the zip fly was worn by the trend-setting Edward, Prince of Wales.

Jeans are the most famous trousers of all. The cloth is a cotton twill, usually blue, which was once made in France. The name denim comes from the French for 'of Nîmes', a French town. Originally made as working men's trousers in the California gold rush, denim jeans are now a universal uniform of youth.

Zips were first used in America to fasten boots. For many years they were unpopular because they were unreliable but by 1918 they were used on flying suits and later on galoshes.

Trousers were worn by the nomads and horsemen of Asia to protect their legs from the cold and stop them getting sore while riding. These trousers probably developed from animal skins that were tied around the legs with thongs.

Many Persian, North Indian and Far Eastern women wear trousers.

Bloomers were an early attempt at women's trousers. They were invented by Amelia Bloomer in 1851 in the interests of health and comfort. She thought them more 'rational' than skirts.

Vietnamese woman

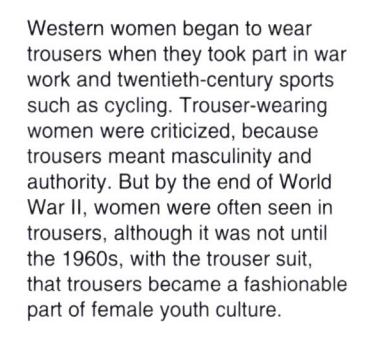

Western women began to wear trousers when they took part in war work and twentieth-century sports such as cycling. Trouser-wearing women were criticized, because trousers meant masculinity and authority. But by the end of World War II, women were often seen in trousers, although it was not until the 1960s, with the trouser suit, that trousers became a fashionable part of female youth culture.

The ancient Romans, in their dignified togas, thought trousers rather barbaric. They only began wearing them after they came into contact with the Celtic and Germanic tribes of the north. Trousers offered better protection against the weather than togas or leather skirts.

In the Middle Ages, men wore hose, a tube-like garment halfway between tights and today's trousers. It was warm and flexible. Around the the same time men started to wear short puffy trousers, gathered at the thigh. They held their hose up by tying it to their shirts with laces called points.

Turn-ups appeared on the bottom of trousers at the end of the nineteenth century. It is said that this trend was started by an Englishman in the United States. He was caught in the rain and late for a wedding, so he turned up his trousers to keep them dry at the bottom, and forgot to turn them down again.

In the late eighteenth century, braces came into use. They kept the front of the breeches smooth and they probably felt comfortable to wear after a large dinner.

After the French Revolution, members of French high society wore long trousers with wide bottoms adopted from the dress of British sailors.

Some sports require special, protective clothing. The first practical aqualung system was devised by Jacques Cousteau and Émile Gagnan in 1943. When added to a pair of flippers, a face mask and a streamlined diving suit, modern scuba diving was born.

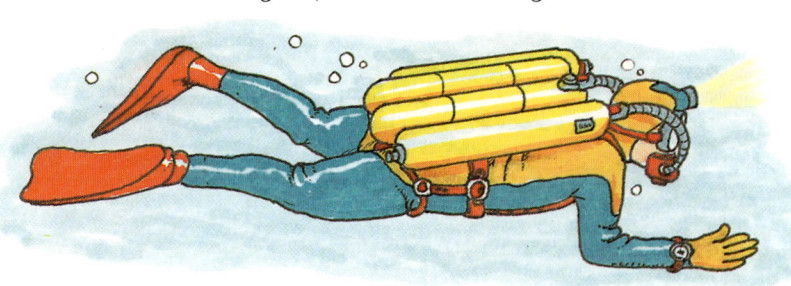

In some sports, players wear bright clothes, sometimes of a special team design, so that team members can be identified. Numbers on the shirt also identify the player. Fans sometimes wear team shirts to show which football club they support.

Looking sporty

Sport has given us many different kinds of clothes. When a sport is new, people tend to use whatever clothes are available, but as time goes by they start to use special items of clothing.

At the beginning of the twentieth century, it was considered indecent to expose too much flesh. Long skirts were worn by women for bathing, cycling, and tennis. However, skirts gradually became much shorter. In 1949, "Gorgeous" Gussie Moran became famous for the short tennis skirts and frilly knickers she wore when she played at Wimbledon.

Sportswear can be attractive enough to wear in everyday life. This is why tennis shoes, jogging suits, baseball caps, and boxer shorts are worn as fashion clothes.

Women's swimming suits used to cover all of the body. They grew shorter and shorter leading eventually to the skimpy two-piece bikini of the 1950s. Strangely enough, a garment like this was originally used by girl gymnasts in Roman times, while ancient Egyptian girl acrobats wore only a loin cloth.

Some materials, such as lycra and sweatshirts, have also come from the world of sport into general use. Sweatshirts are designed to keep you warm when your body cools with sweat. Lycra is an artificial material made from oil. It both stretches and returns to its original shape, keeping a warm, close, comfortable fit.

In sports where people need to move quickly, they use a few, light, close-fitting articles of clothing. The ancient Greeks, who invented the Olympic Games, competed completely naked. These days, some track athletes wear streamlined clothes originally designed for cyclists.

Old-fashioned gear

In some sports, people are still wearing clothes that were fashionable when the sport first became popular. That's why baseball players wear nineteenth-century knickerbockers and socks, for example.

Golf has been played since the 1600s, but it became very popular in the 1920s, and so some of today's golfers wear typical 1920s leisure styles – sweaters, caps, and sometimes knickers.

Protective gear

Atheletes have developed a wide range of protective gear, including leg pads, gloves, and helmets.

Horse riders often wear long boots, breeches or jodhpurs, and a hard hat. Riding breeches are tight at the knee, so the rider can easily grip and guide the horse.

Each of the fighting sports has its own protective clothing. Boxers wear shoes, shorts, and padded mittens, known as boxing gloves. These gloves were introduced by the Marquess of Queensberry in the nineteenth century to make boxing safer.

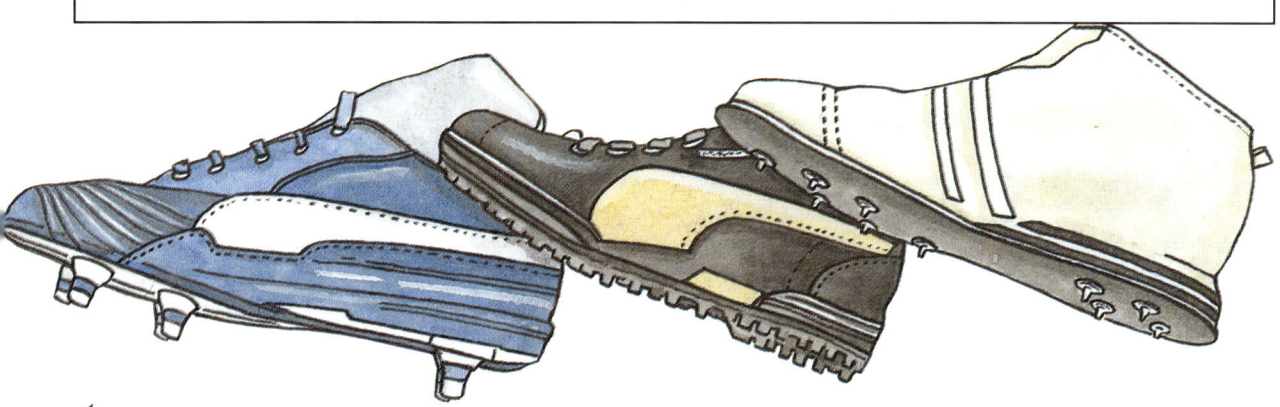

◀ Different sports require different footwear for keeping a grip on the playing surface. Soccer players use different kinds of cleats according to the field. Sprinters use spikes, which were invented by the Romans for marching on rough ground. Some high jumpers use one shoe with spikes and one without.

Jackets, shirts and waistcoats

The modern jacket with a collared shirt and tie beneath, and possibly a waistcoat, is almost like a uniform for Western men. Modern-looking short jackets first appeared in the 1920s. They still retain features from earlier periods that have little use nowadays. ▶

In the 1980s, some women started to wear jackets with padded shoulders. The jackets make women look broader and consequently stronger, maybe helping them to compete with men in business. Clothes with broad shoulders were also worn by women at the turn of this century and during World War II to assert women's equality with men in the workplace.

1900

1943

1985

Button Box

Right- and left-handed buttons: most people are right-handed so men who dressed themselves preferred a button on the right. Wealthy women, on the other hand, were once dressed by their servants, and so buttoning on the left (that is, the servant's right) was more convenient. Button positions have remained ever since.

The lapel buttonhole: coats once buttoned at the neck. People now use it to wear flowers, such as carnations.

The collar slit: collars used to be so high that they would not lie down flat when folded over, unless cut with a slit.

Cuff buttons: cuffs used to be so wide that they had to be buttoned back to stay in place.

A shirt is a type of vest, usually with buttons, which is designed to be seen. It is an ancient garment which has appeared at other times and places, often in longer form, as the tunic (Roman), the caftan (Africa and the East) and the kimono (Japan).

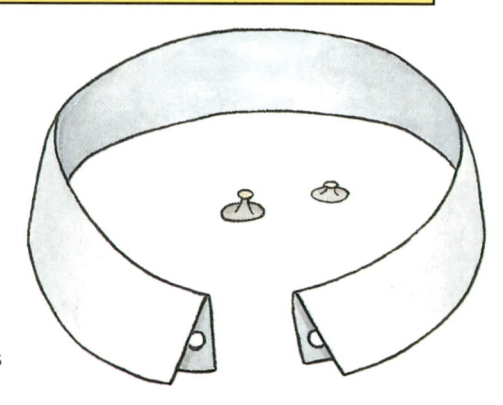

When worn with a coat, some parts of the shirt show at the neck or the sleeves. These parts tend to get dirty, and so, originally, shirt collars and cuffs were separate items that could be changed easily, without having to change the shirt as well.

One cause of the French Revolution, 1789-99, was the extravagant lifestyle of the aristocrats. Because many aristocrats could be recognized by their expensive clothes and had their heads chopped off, it became safer to dress less conspicuously.

Beau Brummel set a new standard of sober elegance for society. The shape of his Regency coat had a great influence on English men's fashion.

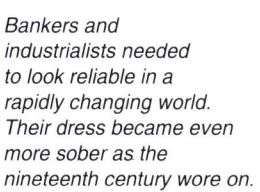

Bankers and industrialists needed to look reliable in a rapidly changing world. Their dress became even more sober as the nineteenth century wore on.

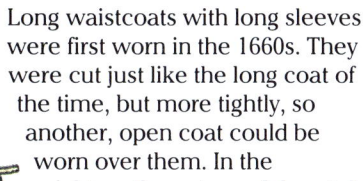

Long waistcoats with long sleeves were first worn in the 1660s. They were cut just like the long coat of the time, but more tightly, so another, open coat could be worn over them. In the eighteenth century, elaborately embroidered waistcoats could reach down to the knee. Today, only the short waistcoat survives, normally as part of a three-piece suit. Sometimes a lavishly coloured silk waistcoat is still worn.

For most of European history, men's fashions were often more splendid than women's, just as among animals the males are often more brightly coloured than the females. The modern, sober style of dress for men was introduced in the nineteenth century.

In cold weather a long- or short-sleeved pullover may be worn over the shirt, and under a jacket. Pullovers are really just overshirts made of wool for warmth.

Pullover, 1935

American bomber jacket, 1945

Anorak, 1960

If you want to show that you belong in a certain group, you can wear a blazer – striped or just one colour, often with a badge on the breast pocket. They are thought to have been worn first by the crew of the Royal Navy ship HMS *Blazer* in 1845.

The leather, fleece-lined jacket worn by World War II bomber crews has made a big impact on post-war styles. The bomber jacket was redesigned by motorcyclists, and the new biker's jacket was made famous by Marlon Brando in the 1954 film *The Wild One*. The grubby leather jacket is now often seen as a symbol of youthful rebellion.

Anoraks were originally Inuit garments made of seal skin.

SUIT YOURSELF

Today's suit was an invention of the twentieth century, though its origins were much earlier. By the 1920s, men were no longer expected to express themselves in their dress. Individual tailoring went into decline. Men began to buy their suits more cheaply with 'off the peg' standard designs.

By the middle of the nineteenth century, men's outerwear had settled down to three main pieces – a cut-away coat, a waistcoat and the newly adopted trousers. At first, the three pieces would be of different colours, favourites for everyday wear being London Fog, Algerian Dust and Russian Green. But after 1850, only the waistcoat remained colourful. The age of the businessman had begun and sober colours reflected the sombre style of the City of London.

Business suit, 1870

Since World War II, the grey suit has been increasingly restricted to business and formal wear. The English man's suit, as designed by Hardy Amies and manufactured in Savile Row, remains a classic.

Business suit, 1960

In the 1980s, the Milan-based designer, Giorgio Armani, began to produce looser, baggier suits. They could be worn with the sleeves pushed up, as by pop star George Michael.

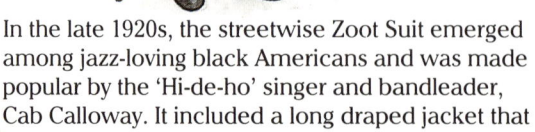

In the late 1920s, the streetwise Zoot Suit emerged among jazz-loving black Americans and was made popular by the 'Hi-de-ho' singer and bandleader, Cab Calloway. It included a long draped jacket that reached the knee, vast shoulder pads and baggy trousers that tapered at the turn-ups. It was worn with pointed shoes, a broad-brimmed hat, a lengthy, dangling key-chain and long greased-back hair.

The Zazou fashion of post-war Paris was based on the Zoot Suit but had drooping shoulders and tight trousers. In the 1950s, the Teddy Boy style continued the draped coat tradition, but added thick crêpe-soled shoes and, for the hair, a quiff, swept-back sides and sideburns. Teddy girls wore less distinctive clothes but were recognizable by their pony tails.

Neckwear has changed steadily over the centuries.

The Elizabethan ruff, 1575

The soft lace collar, 1635

The neckcloth, 1795

The cravat, 1840

The bow tie, 1890

The modern tie is normally tied with a four-in-hand knot, although the fatter Windsor knot was made fashionable by the Duke of Windsor.

The necktie, 1913

Around 1800, Beau Brummel, the leader of Regency fashion, advised the Prince Regent to wear black or dark blue coats for evening wear. Evening knee-breeches were already usually black at that time, so when trousers were introduced they too were black. The black evening suit was born. By about 1870, the full evening dress tail-coat suit was well established. These days, the long-tailed evening dress suit is normally only worn by posh waiters. However, a similar morning dress survives at modern weddings, though these suits are usually coloured light grey.

Today's short, modern dinner jacket came into use at the start of the twentieth century. For a time it was thought too informal for dining out, because tail-coats were still worn. By the 1920s, however, short jackets were accepted for formal evening wear.

In the late nineteenth century an attempt was made to go back to the fancier clothes of earlier times. The 'Little Lord Fauntleroy' suit worn by some nineteenth-century children was based on Thomas Gainsborough's 1770 painting, *The Blue Boy*. Oscar Wilde tried to popularize it as men's wear and wore it on a tour of America, but it didn't catch on.

17

POSH DRESSES

Original tailored dresses are very expensive, but designers also create simpler, less expensive versions which they sell 'off the peg' in dress shops under their own labels. This trend followed the mass-market success of popular designers such as Mary Quant in the 1960s.

Court dress, 1865

Wedding dress worn by Lady Diana Spencer, 1981

For hundreds of years, until early in the twentieth century, women's dresses generally grew more and more lavish, getting larger, more complex, and using more and more material. Women not only wanted to look more attractive but also to show off their wealth and position.

In the Middle Ages in Europe, dresses were still fairly simple. Fabric was expensive and status was shown by the cost of the material, fur trim or jewels that went with it. It was against the law in some countries for lower class people to wear expensive clothing.

By the fifteenth century, the skirts of dresses were made so long and full they had to be held up as the lady moved. This resulted in a big bunching of material in front so that the woman often looked as if she was pregnant even when she wasn't.

Late in the sixteenth century, women started wearing various types of structure under the skirt, such as bumrolls, bustles or crinolines. This meant that even more material could be used but the wearer could still just about move with them.

The French Revolution not only abolished the monarchy but also the extravagant style of dresses of the French royal court. Clothes became simple and based on classical Greek clothing. To make dresses cling the way they did in classical sculptures, the dresses were sometimes worn damp. As houses in those days were not well heated, some young women literally died of cold.

Modern dress styles were really introduced in the 1920s, when designer Coco Chanel started a dress revolution. By making a simple, straight dress with a short skirt reaching just below the knee, she allowed young women to go more easily to work, dance and take part in sports. Since then, there have been numerous variations in the length and fullness of dresses.

Late eighteenth-century posh dresses were remarkable for their complexity and elegance.

Extravagant, complicated costume, 1790

Special clothes or materials were traded round the world and often named after the places they came from. For example cambric linen came from Cambrai in France, suede leather came from Sweden and cashmere wool came from Kashmir on the Indian subcontinent.

The Paisley pattern originally came from the East, and the 'comma' shapes were created by stamping the dye onto the cloth with the side of the fist. Later a factory was set up in Paisley, Scotland, to produce the cloth industrially.

During World War II, women were encouraged to wear simple dresses that saved material.

Dresses with short skirts and bright colours were designed by Mary Quant, who helped to create the 1960s 'dolly bird'. 'Dolly birds' tended to be very slim with eyes made up to look large.

Famous Names

The modern dress-making industry is a vast enterprise. At the top are great designers whose original creations are displayed by top models in Paris and other major cities. Famous twentieth-century designers include Charles Worth, Jean Poiret, Coco Chanel, Christian Dior, Yves St Laurent, Barbara Hulanicki, Jean Muir, Mary Quant and Vivienne Westwood.

19

UNIFORMS

A uniform makes a group of otherwise quite different individuals look similar. It is a simple way to make sure that everyone in a group is dressed both smartly and suitably. It also helps us to know what people do. For instance, if someone becomes seriously ill at a football match, someone who can help needs to be found quickly. That's why ambulance staff wear a uniform that people will recognize.

Until the middle of the last century, many soldiers wore brightly-coloured uniforms. Red was popular because it is a bold, threatening colour and hides blood stains. Unfortunately bright colours made soldiers easy targets. In 1843, Harry Lumsden, a British officer in India, issued his men in the Queen's Own Corps of Guides with cotton clothing dyed grey with mazari, a local plant. The leather items were dyed with mulberry juice to produce a drab yellow shade, called 'khaki' after the local word for dust. In 1849, these Guides, known as 'mudlarks', were seen in battle for the first time. Except for ceremonial occasions, most soldiers now wear dull colours or camouflage uniforms.

US Army jungle camouflage uniform, 1945

Military uniforms may include elements designed to make the soldier look fiercer. Hats and vertical stripes make people seem taller. Fur and feather head-dresses suggest a fierce animal with its hair on end. Frogging or gold braid in rows across the body may have come from an ancient custom of going into battle painted like a skeleton to scare the enemy.

Zulu warrior, 1879

Trumpeter, French Imperial Guard, 1810

A uniform can give the idea that the wearer is prepared to serve others. Because the uniform makes the wearer more anonymous we may find it easier to ask them to do things for us. That is one reason why shop assistants often wear special clothes.

Different military ranks wear different uniforms or insignia so that an easily recognized chain of command is maintained. Chevrons are worn on the arm by some British Army ranks. ▼

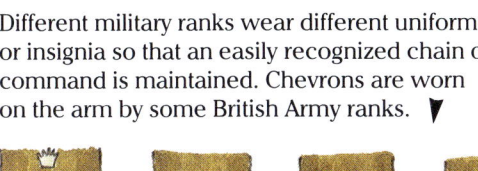

Staff sergeant   Sergeant   Corporal   Lance corporal   Private

Dungaree was a coarse, Indian blue, calico material used for sails. After a bad storm, sailors sometimes used any ripped sails to make new trousers. This became part of a sailor's outfit. With the addition of a bib in front, they became the modern form of dungarees. ▶

In the Middle Ages, doctors wore gowns of blue and red to hide the blood. Today the academic gowns worn in some universities still preserve these colours, as well as the medieval gown, hood or cap.

Before the introduction of ▶ purpose-built hospitals, nursing was often performed by nuns. The traditional nurse's uniforms are developed from the nuns' cape, cloak and headwear.

Augustinian nursing sister, 1256

Parlourmaid, 1893

Nurse, 1905

The traditional posh waitress's uniform of black with a white apron is a development of the nineteenth-century parlourmaid's outfit.

School uniforms in many parts of the world are based on the English boarding-school uniforms of the 1920s. They often include blazers with a badge. Some boys still wear caps, whereas girls wear round felt or straw hats. ▶

Traditional school uniforms

21

OVERCOATS AND GLOVES

The overcoat is an answer to an age-old problem – what to wear if you go out in rainy or cold weather. Wearing thick clothes was fine but if they were wet through you would either have to sit in them when you got home or change them. With an overcoat, you could simply take the outer garment off.

The first overcoats were long, cut-away jackets made of tough material. During the eighteenth century, coach travel became more and more commonplace. People who rode on top were exposed to the weather for long periods. They needed heavy great-coats with large collars.

By the beginning of the eighteenth century, women in England were able to wear lightweight walking coats outside their simpler, straighter gowns. Soon the race was on to develop a truly waterproof coat.

Charles Macintosh was a nineteenth-century chemist who produced a kind of waterproof smock lined with rubber. This was called a mackintosh. Early mackintoshes sometimes smelled very bad and caused offense.

Some modern mackintoshes are made of transparent plastic and bright, shiny PVC. Increasingly, people are wearing shorter types of rainwear as, with modern transport, they do not expect to be in bad weather much of the time.

Barbour coat

In the eighteenth century, waterproofs were made of tarpaulin (sail-cloth coated with tar), or oil-cloth (a cloth coated with boiled linseed oil). Today's Barbour country coat is descended from these first waterproof coats.

Fur has been worn from earliest times for warmth, and also as a luxury item. It is less popular today as many people think that animals should not die to provide luxurious clothes for people.

The modern anorak, or parka, was originally an Inuit garment made from fur turned inside out for warmth. For a fully waterproof garment, the Inuit cured fish skins and sewed them together.

The cape or cloak was simple and could be worn easily on horseback. One version of the cape that is widely worn today is the South American poncho, a blanket used by gaucho cowboys.

Glove Box

Gloves were an important item of clothing in the Middle Ages and often had a symbolic value. To give your hand or glove meant to pledge your loyalty, while throwing your glove at an enemy was a way of challenging him or her to a duel.

In the sixteenth and seventeenth centuries, richly embroidered gloves were given as valuable presents.

Women began to wear shorter-sleeved dresses in the 1630s, but they also wore gloves that reached the elbow.

Another way of keeping warm is to wear a muff. By the eighteenth century, muffs had grown big enough to carry lap-dogs in and were sometimes worn by men. They became an important fashion accessory and by 1880, muffs were sometimes worn with the heads of owls or squirrels attached. Some were made of the entire body of a kitten!

During the late nineteenth century it was thought indecent for women to show too much skin. They would often wear lace or net gloves – even indoors.

23

For hundreds of years in many parts of the world, fair skin was the mark of a lady of leisure. It proved that she didn't have to work outside in the sunlight. In the twentieth century this has changed. A tanned skin is evidence of a long sunny holiday. It has become a sign of wealth, and so is thought attractive. This is why some people wear fake suntan, or lie under a sun-lamp, to look darker. On the other hand, it is now known that too much exposure to the Sun can cause skin cancer and it is no longer thought unfashionable to have white skin.

From Roman times, European ladies have used special substances to whiten their skins. However, in the sixteenth century, rouge was also applied to add colour to the cheeks.

The ancient Egyptians used both orange and yellow face paints. Egyptian women liked to look light and so tended to use yellow; Egyptian men wanted to look dark and so used only orange. Cleopatra also used varnish on her nails.

MAKE-UP, HAIR AND TATTOOS

Even the finest clothes don't make a person happy if he or she thinks there's something wrong with the way they look. People have always gone to great lengths to change their eyes, lips, skin and hair.

One special kind of body decoration is the tattoo. This is a body pattern created by injecting a dark dye under the skin wherever the pattern is wanted. An extreme form of tattooing is practised by the Maoris of New Zealand. European sailors came across the habit in many parts of the world and often had their own tattoos made. Tattooing became very popular in the late nineteenth century.

Maori face tattoos

Celtic warrior, 55 BC

Tattoos don't show up well on people with very dark skin so they use the keloid or scarring technique. This is a common practice in Africa. The skin is cut or pierced repeatedly, then left to heal, leaving a slightly raised scar pattern.

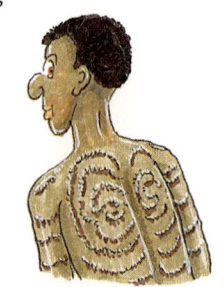

The Celts, who lived in much of western Europe, used to decorate their bodies. When Julius Caesar arrived in Britain, he found that Celtic warriors sometimes painted themselves with a blue vegetable dye called woad. This may have been to protect themselves magically or to make them look frightening.

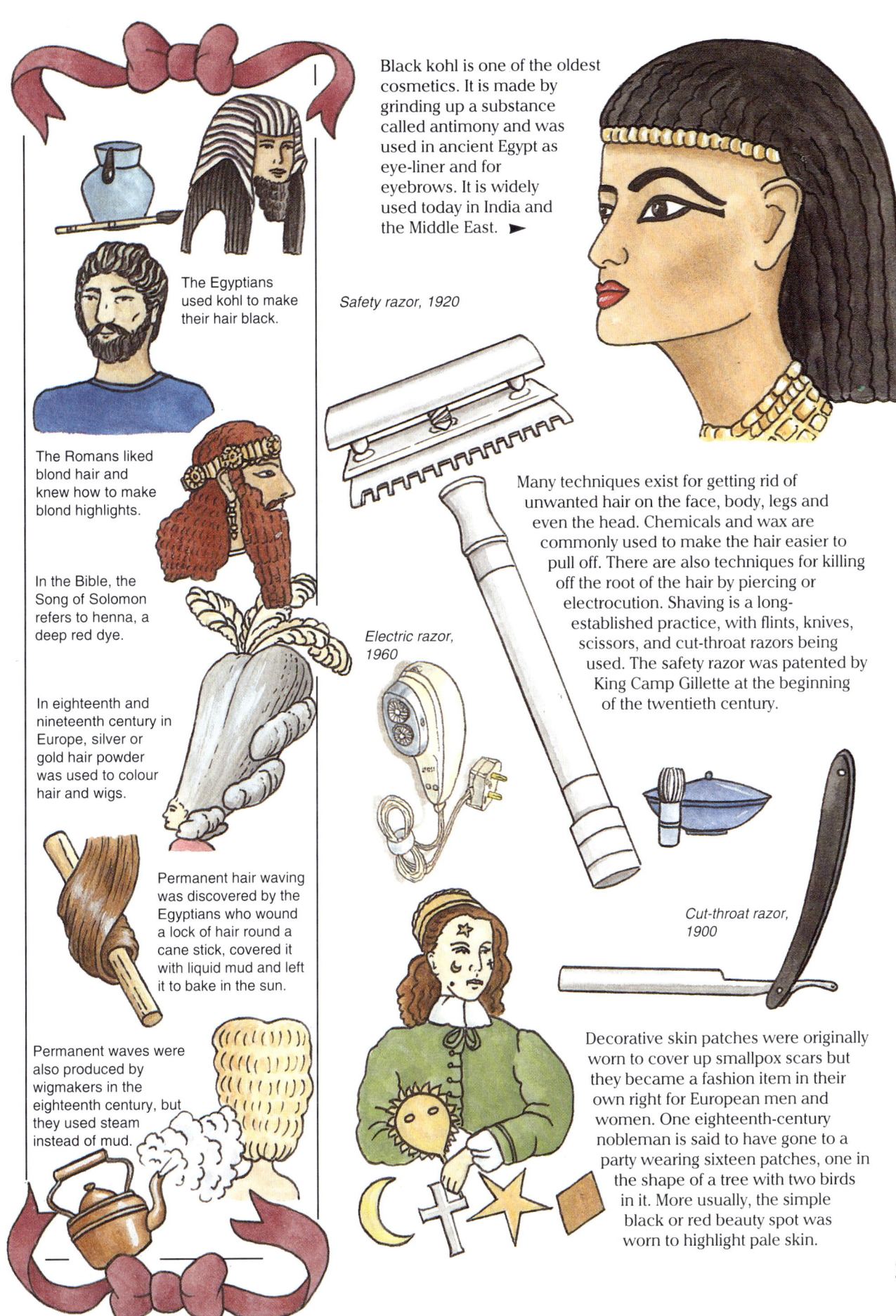

Black kohl is one of the oldest cosmetics. It is made by grinding up a substance called antimony and was used in ancient Egypt as eye-liner and for eyebrows. It is widely used today in India and the Middle East.

The Egyptians used kohl to make their hair black.

The Romans liked blond hair and knew how to make blond highlights.

In the Bible, the Song of Solomon refers to henna, a deep red dye.

In eighteenth and nineteenth century in Europe, silver or gold hair powder was used to colour hair and wigs.

Permanent hair waving was discovered by the Egyptians who wound a lock of hair round a cane stick, covered it with liquid mud and left it to bake in the sun.

Permanent waves were also produced by wigmakers in the eighteenth century, but they used steam instead of mud.

Safety razor, 1920

Electric razor, 1960

Many techniques exist for getting rid of unwanted hair on the face, body, legs and even the head. Chemicals and wax are commonly used to make the hair easier to pull off. There are also techniques for killing off the root of the hair by piercing or electrocution. Shaving is a long-established practice, with flints, knives, scissors, and cut-throat razors being used. The safety razor was patented by King Camp Gillette at the beginning of the twentieth century.

Cut-throat razor, 1900

Decorative skin patches were originally worn to cover up smallpox scars but they became a fashion item in their own right for European men and women. One eighteenth-century nobleman is said to have gone to a party wearing sixteen patches, one in the shape of a tree with two birds in it. More usually, the simple black or red beauty spot was worn to highlight pale skin.

25

Jewels and Things

People have been using ornaments, umbrellas and handbags for thousands of years. Personal ornaments are probably an older tradition than clothes. Why do we decorate ourselves in this way? Is it to look beautiful or wealthy? Or for reasons of magic, religion or superstition? Sometimes it is simply because we need to carry something useful with us!

Jewels are made from attractive stones or metals that are often of great value because they are hard to find. Rare jewels show how rich the wearer is.

Some people suffer great discomfort for their ideas of beauty. In one African tribe, women stretch the neck by placing as many neck-rings as possible around it. This is because a long neck is often considered a sign of beauty. Neck-stretching is also practised in Myanmar (formerly Burma).

After the French Revolution, women offset their simple, low-cut dresses by wearing a red ribbon around the neck. This was a reference to the guillotine, the machine that was used to cut off the heads of the king's supporters.

The ancient Aztecs of Central America wore nose and ear ornaments made of gold. When attending festivals, they wore face paints and stamped patterns on their cheeks.

In medieval and Tudor times, heavy gold chains and ropes of pearls could be used as a substitute for money, with a length being broken off, weighed for its value and used as cash. Jewellery of different kinds has been used as money in this way because it has value and yet is easy to carry.

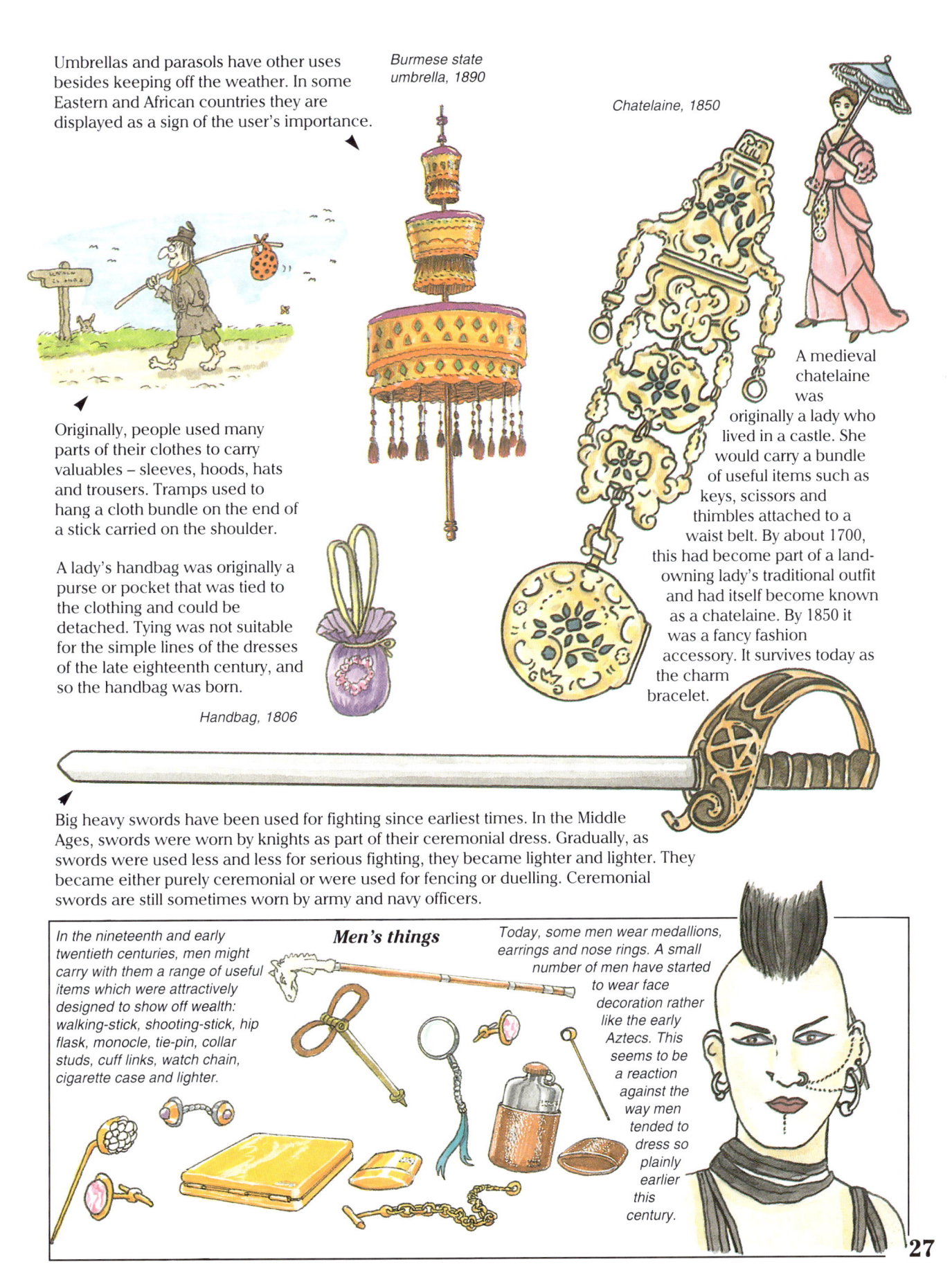

Umbrellas and parasols have other uses besides keeping off the weather. In some Eastern and African countries they are displayed as a sign of the user's importance.

Burmese state umbrella, 1890

Chatelaine, 1850

Originally, people used many parts of their clothes to carry valuables – sleeves, hoods, hats and trousers. Tramps used to hang a cloth bundle on the end of a stick carried on the shoulder.

A lady's handbag was originally a purse or pocket that was tied to the clothing and could be detached. Tying was not suitable for the simple lines of the dresses of the late eighteenth century, and so the handbag was born.

Handbag, 1806

A medieval chatelaine was originally a lady who lived in a castle. She would carry a bundle of useful items such as keys, scissors and thimbles attached to a waist belt. By about 1700, this had become part of a land-owning lady's traditional outfit and had itself become known as a chatelaine. By 1850 it was a fancy fashion accessory. It survives today as the charm bracelet.

Big heavy swords have been used for fighting since earliest times. In the Middle Ages, swords were worn by knights as part of their ceremonial dress. Gradually, as swords were used less and less for serious fighting, they became lighter and lighter. They became either purely ceremonial or were used for fencing or duelling. Ceremonial swords are still sometimes worn by army and navy officers.

Men's things

In the nineteenth and early twentieth centuries, men might carry with them a range of useful items which were attractively designed to show off wealth: walking-stick, shooting-stick, hip flask, monocle, tie-pin, collar studs, cuff links, watch chain, cigarette case and lighter.

Today, some men wear medallions, earrings and nose rings. A small number of men have started to wear face decoration rather like the early Aztecs. This seems to be a reaction against the way men tended to dress so plainly earlier this century.

27

Because hats are connected with power, men have often worn tall hats, and the more powerful the man, the larger the hat. People of lower status have usually worn smaller hats, taking them off in the presence of someone of higher rank. Traditionally, men also take off their hats in church and when meeting women. Women's hats are usually more decorative and fashionable than men's practical hats.

Choosing a hat

Gentleman taking of his hat, 1908

Wimple

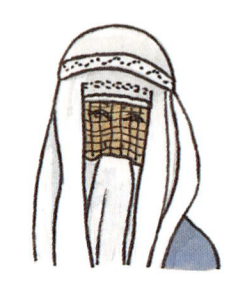

Yashmak

European women hardly wore hats at all until the sixteenth century. Headwear was often an elaborate veil or headscarf. In the Middle Ages, women wore a wimple – a piece of cloth covering the head. The wimple survives among nuns and nurses to the present day. Following upper class Greek practice in ancient Byzantium, many Muslim women now cover their faces with veils or face screens known as yashmaks.

Flat cap

Fez

Though baseball caps are popular these days, it's not fashionable in the West for men to wear traditional hats. In very cold or very hot weather, however, hats provide the wearer with shelter. They keep the head warm in winter and cool in summer.

▼ Government regulations in Elizabethan times said that middle-ranking men should wear flat caps – a tradition that continued until the mid-twentieth century among working class men.

▼ In some Muslim countries, men have worn turbans in a great variety of styles. Some have been copied by women in the West as fashion items. Some Muslim men also wear the fez, although in the 1920s this was banned in Turkey as part of an effort to make Turkey more Westernized.

The Mad Hatter's hat, 1865

Felt is a material made by soaking and compressing wool or fur so that the fibres bind together into a kind of matting. It is often used to make hats because it can be shaped easily. The best felt used to come from old and sweaty beaver furs that had been worn by Russian noblemen.

▼ In the eighteenth century, hat makers started to use mercuric nitrate as part of the felt-making process, without realizing that it was a poison. As a result, many hatters became mentally ill because their nerves were affected. Lewis Carroll, the author of *Alice in Wonderland*, based the character of the Mad Hatter on this affliction.

Hats come in all shapes and sizes.

The wide brim of the Mexican sombrero provides enough shade to cover the whole body.

The big, woolly hats worn by some Rastafarians keep their hair covered and bunched.

The balaclava is named after the woolly head-covers knitted for British soldiers who fought in the Battle of Balaklava, 1854.

The boater is a flat straw hat worn in the Victorian period by people who went boating on summer afternoons.

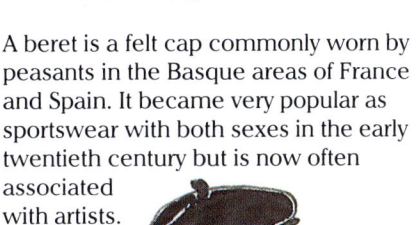

The Lapland bonnet has four pointed corners. Three can be stuffed with feathers for use as a pillow and the other used as a pocket or a purse.

Hat Box

A range of brimmed hats were worn by men in the nineteenth and early twentieth centuries.

Top hat

Stetson

Trilby

Bowler

Homburg

A beret is a felt cap commonly worn by peasants in the Basque areas of France and Spain. It became very popular as sportswear with both sexes in the early twentieth century but is now often associated with artists.

In the Australian bush, corks dangling from hat brims help to keep the flies away.

29

Men sometimes wear small hair pieces, or toupees, to disguise baldness. They are mostly knotted to a piece of netting and fixed to the scalp with double-sided tape.

Hair today, gone tomorrow!

Other techniques of fighting baldness include implanting live hairs from elsewhere on the scalp, weaving hair into the scalp, and even cutting out the bald sections of the flesh over the skull and joining up the hairy parts.

WIGS

Some people wear wigs because they are bald – but that's never been the only reason for wearing them. Quite often people like to wear wigs for reasons of fashion. They are especially handy when the hairstyle required is a complicated one. Wigs can be made from human hair or from artificial fibres.

In the seventeenth and eighteenth centuries, the wig became an essential item for fashionable men and women. Its height and complexity increased to absurd proportions.

Afro wigs imitated a black hairstyle. In the late 1960s, it was popular with some white people who wanted to show solidarity with the struggle for black civil rights.

Roman women's fashion demanded a wardrobe of wigs. Golden Germanic hair was very popular.

The ancient Egyptians shaved their heads for coolness, but wore heavy wigs on formal occasions.

◀ English lawyers still use wigs of the eighteenth-century style.

Toupee – or not toupee!

In eighteenth-century Europe, wigs became so popular that it was dangerous for children to go out alone in case their hair was cut off and stolen. Some bold thieves even stole expensive wigs!

30

WILLY AND WANDA'S WACKYWEAR

QUIZ — WHY DO WE?

Willy and Wanda have been invited to a '1796 Fancy Dress Ball'. Unfortunately the fancy dress shop has run out of the proper items. They each could only find three things worn in Europe in 1796. Do you know which they are?

Willy's items:
- Homburg
- Balaclava
- Beauty spot
- Ruff
- Necktie
- T-shirt
- Braces
- Mackintosh smock
- Roman skirt
- Breeches
- Wellies

Wanda's items:
- Fez
- Gold-powdered wig
- Aqualung
- Red neck-ribbon
- Jacket with padded shoulders
- Muffs
- Bustle
- Zip-up handbag
- Fishtail skirt
- Nylons
- Poulaines

ANSWERS:

WILLY – Beauty spot (see page 25), Braces (see page 11), Breeches (see page 10)

WANDA – Gold-powdered wig (see page 30), Red neck-ribbon (see page 26), Muffs (see page 23)

INDEX

Anorak 15, 23
Apron 21
Aqualung 12

Bell bottoms 10, 11
Bikini 12
Blazer 15, 21
Bloomers 7, 11
Bomber jacket 15
Boots 5, 13
Bow tie 17
Boxer shorts 7, 12
Bra 6, 12
Braces 11
Breeches 10, 11, 13
Bustle 7, 18
Button 7, 10, 14

Caftan 14
Cap 12, 13, 21, 28
Cape 21, 23
Cloak 21, 23
Clogs 5
Coat 14-17, 22
Collar 14, 17, 22
Corset 6, 7
Cravat 17
Crinolines 7, 18
Cuffs 11, 14

Dhoti 8
Dinner jacket 17
Diving suit 12
Drainpipe trousers 10
Drawers 7
Dress 18, 19, 26
Dungarees 21

Epiblemata 3

Fashion designers 9, 19
Fez 28
Flares 10
Flying suit 10

Gaiters 5
Galoshes 5, 10
Garters 6
Girdle 6
Gloves 13, 23
Gown 21, 22
Grass skirt 9

Haik 8
Handbag 26, 27
Hat 13, 20, 21, 27-29
Headscarf 28
Helmet 13
High heels 25

Hipsters 10
Hood 21, 27
Hose 11

Insoles 4

Jacket 14-17, 22
Jeans 10
Jewels 18, 26
Jodhpurs 13

Keloid technique 24
Kilt 8
Kimono 14
Knickerbockers 10, 13
Knickers 7, 12

Liberty bodice 7
Loincloth 12
Loons 10

Mackintosh 22
Make-up 24-27
Mini-skirt 9
Muffs 23

Neckcloth 17
Neck-rings 26
Necktie 17

'Off the peg' 16
Opanques 4
Overcoat 22
Oxford bags 10

Padded shoulders 14, 16
Parasol 27
Parka 23
Petticoat 7
Pleat 8
Plus fours 13
Pocket 15, 27, 29
Poulaines 5
Poncho 23
Pullover 15
Purse 29

Revival 2, 10
Robe 21
Ruff 17

Sabots 5
Sandals 4
Sari 8
Sarong 8
Shirt 12, 14, 15

Shoes 4, 5, 13, 16
Shorts 13
Singlet 6
Skirt 8, 9, 11, 12, 18
Slacks 6
Sneakers 5
Socks 6, 13
Sportswear 11-13, 29
Stiletto heels 5
Stockings 6, 10, 11
Studs 13
Suit 15-17
Sun tan 24
Suspenders 6
Sweater 7, 13
Sword 23

Tail-coat 17
Tailoring 16, 18
Tattoo 24
Three-piece suit 15
Tie 14, 17
Tights 9, 11
Toga 11
Track suit 12
Train 9
Trainers 5, 12
Trousers 10, 11, 17, 21, 27
Trouser suit 11
T-shirt 6
Tunic 14
Turban 28
Turn-ups 11

Umbrella 26
Underwear 6, 7
Uniform 14, 20, 21
Unisex 2

Veil 28
Vest 6, 14

Waistcoat 14-16
Wedding dress 18
Wellington boots 5
Wig 25, 30
Wimple 28
Winklepickers 5
Woad 24

Yashmak 28
Y-fronts 6

Zazou 16
Zip 10
Zoot Suit 16

First published in 1996 by
Franklin Watts
96 Leonard Street
London
EC2A 4RH

Franklin Watts Australia
14 Mars Road
Lane Cove
NSW 2060

ISBN: 0 7496 1907 4

A CIP catalogue record for this book is available from the British Library.
Dewey Decimal Classification: 391

© 1996 Lazy Summer Books Ltd
Illustrated by Lazy Summer Books Ltd
   and Denise Heywood
Printed in Belgium